THE Entrepreneurs
SUCCESS AND SACRIFICE

BY KIP MARLOW

ISBN: 1482023830
ISBN-13: 9781482023831
Library of Congress Control Number: 2013901206
CreateSpace Independent Publishing Platform
North Charleston, South Carolina

Pre-Publishing Praise for
The Entrepreneurs: Success and Sacrifice

March 20, 2013

"A great group of inspiring stories about successful businesses you can actually identify with. Any business owner or entrepreneur who has ever had a dark moment will feel pumped up and motivated after reading *The Entrepreneurs: Success and Sacrifice.*"

Anita Campbell, Publisher, *Small Business Trends*

"I enjoyed the book very much. It's a great collection of inspiration, perspiration, dedication, hard work, and a little fun too! This would be great to read after a tough day of growing your business or as a way to see if you have what it takes to get a chapter written about you! I highly recommend this one."

Jim Beach, Co-Author of *The School for Startups* and Host of School for Start-ups Radio. Atlanta, Georgia

"All small-business owners need to read this book to help them understand that they are not alone! Others have experienced the pain, suffering, hardship, and joy of starting and growing a business and overcame great odds. When you read the stories in this book, you will be inspired, motivated, and supercharged because you will understand that you can do what they did as well!"

Ron Finklestein, International Author, Speaker, Business Growth Specialist

"Hard work, discipline, and perseverance are the ingredients of success. You can find them all and much more in the stories that Kip Marlow tells in *The Entrepreneurs: Success and Sacrifice*. This book contains real-world stories of men and women who have succeeded against the odds in building thriving businesses. Their commitment, often at great hardship, is sure to teach as well as inspire."

John Baldoni, executive coach, leadership educator, and author of *Lead with Purpose* and *The Leader's Pocket Guide*

"A must read for anyone contemplating life as an entrepreneur. A beautiful journey down memory lane for those of us already afflicted."

Robert Brian Johnson, author of *Into the Black*

"From one story to the next, *The Entrepreneurs: Success and Sacrifice* inspires and motivates. Reading the journeys to success of real-world entrepreneurs reminds us that as long as we believe and are willing to think creatively, we too can reach the pinnacle of our dreams. This book is essential for all business owners aspiring to make it big—whatever 'big' means to them."

Diane Helbig, author of *Lemonade Stand Selling*, business advisor, and radio host of Accelerate Your Business Growth

FOREWORD

Type As. ADDs. PhDs. High School Dropouts. Risk-takers. Panic attack victims.

How do you define entrepreneurs? For generations, writers have defined them scientifically or psychologically. Most often, they have defined them from a business perspective. Kip Marlow has attacked this challenge differently. He has interviewed hundreds of entrepreneurs, some at the top, some still climbing, some on the other side. And these are their stories...not distorted by some message Kip wanted to share—these are purely *their stories*. And since he is an entrepreneur and knows how busy we all are, he doesn't waste our time with frivolous details. The pertinent facts are all that we need to get the message, allowing us to understand a little better how entrepreneurs each overcome inevitable obstacles on their way to the top.

Kip shared an early version of this book so I could author this foreword. As a busy entrepreneur who has already read countless business books and, in my radio career, interviewed many successful local and international entrepreneurs, I expected to quickly scan a few pages from each chapter and then start writing.

To my surprise, I had to read every word of every chapter. There was just too much "meat and potatoes" here, and too much personality...from the entrepreneurs and from Kip. Interesting? Yes. Fascinating? Indeed. Inspirational? Absolutely!

For anyone who already knows he or she is an entrepreneur, or thinks he or she might be one, these stories are a *must read*. I found it especially interesting that some stories are about millionaires, and some feature people still trying to get there—although I sure wouldn't bet against any of them. So especially for you who are frustrated by your current predicament or unsure that you should take the plunge and leave a supposedly secure career, you will definitely be inspired by the way these entrepreneurs have been persistent in avoiding the temptation of staying in or returning to their comfort zones.

I predict that this book will spawn hundreds, perhaps thousands of new entrepreneurs...and recharge thousands more who temporarily misplaced the passion that started them on their special journey. There could not be a better time for this book, because the country and the world need entrepreneurs more than ever. Maybe you will discover that this book was really written just for *you.*

Kip wrote it. I loved it. We both hope you will too.

Ray Somich
President, Spirit Media
& co-owner of WELW Radio

TABLE OF CONTENTS

CHAPTER 1
Kip Marlow

*Can Anyone
Be An Entrepreneur?*

Probably not. It takes a certain mindset, a vision, lots of patience and persistence, and yes, hard work. It doesn't take a Harvard MBA or a ton of money. In some cases, it doesn't even take a college degree, but it sure helps.

The Entrepreneurs is about twenty-two different people, interviewed on Entrepreneurs Club Radio, who started their businesses in different industries and mostly for different reasons. Some had a dream to create something of value. One was a banker who took the plunge into entrepreneurship. One never graduated from high school, grew up in poverty, and wanted to get out of the ghetto. At least one was laid off from her job and found that it "was the door that opened wide." In each instance a new company was born.

As you read each chapter, watch for what challenges these twenty-two entrepreneurs had to overcome, the risks they took, and what they learned from their experiences. Understand their lessons learned and secrets of success and try to apply them to your dream businesses.

If you are an entrepreneur and wish to grow your business, you will glean valuable information and be inspired by each of these wonderful stories. If deep down you are someone that always wanted to follow your passion and start a business, this book will inspire, encourage, and teach some of the fundamentals needed to succeed.

It has often been said that facts tell and stories sell, so we chose stories. This book isn't three hundred pages on how to write a business plan or read financial statements. These stories are about under the radar small business owners who had the courage, focus, and where-with-all to start their enterprises and build value for their employees, their families, and themselves.

Read. Learn. Enjoy!

CHAPTER 2
Scott Marincek
Founder of Solv-All

*Blowing Up
His Mother's Blender*

My mom said, "What the heck are you doing with my blender?" I said, "Mom this is going to solve everyone's problems." She replied, "You better solve me a new blender."

—Scott Marincek

Scott Marincek is a dreamer who is always trying to envision the end result of his many projects. He also loves the game of basketball. For the past twenty years, he has combined the team concepts he sees in the game of basketball with dreaming. The result is Solv-All, a company that specializes in cleaning products and services.

Scott enjoys helping people. When he started the company, his intention was to provide hardworking people with jobs that would allow them to be successful. Solv-All was established to offer environmentally preferable products and services to its customers. Today, it provides cleaning products and services to retailers across the country, including Target, Sears, JC Penny, and Kmart.

Let's back up to 1990. Scott is fresh out of high school. He decides that he wants to be an emergency medical technician, so he enrolls at the local community college to take the classes and get his license. To pay the bills along the way, Scott takes a job mixing cleaning chemicals for a local janitorial supply company. The minimum wage work allows him the flexibility to get the classes he will need to become an EMT.

The work was simple enough. Scott just mixed chemicals in the back of a distribution facility. He noticed that a lot of the chemicals that went into the cleaning solutions either weren't safe for the user or weren't environmentally friendly. Some of the chemicals he was mixing seemed to be downright dangerous. Were these compounds absolutely necessary?

There had to be a product on the market that was safer both for the person using it and for the environment. Scott did a little research and found, to his amazement, that there wasn't such a model.

The next day, he knocked on the company owner's door and asked him why they couldn't make a cleaning product that was not only environmentally safer but also was less dangerous for the user and performed as well as its unsafe counterparts. The

"Scott, you'll never make it in business because you're too honest and too nice."

response he received was certainly not one that he had expected. Laughing at him, the owner said, "Scott, you'll never make it in business because you're too honest and too nice."

The owner went on and on about how using the questionable chemical in several different products was better for marketing and overall sales. Not enough people would care about environmentally safe cleaners, let alone buy them.

Undeterred, Scott took home samples of the raw material ingredients and blew up his mother's kitchen. Well, not literally...but it sure seemed that way. Scott knew that he could combine some different and safer ingredients to make cleaning products that would ease his conscience. Since he had no budget and no laboratory, Scott was relegated to experimenting on his new formula in his parents' kitchen.

One day, while his mother was out working in the yard, Scott was experimenting with possible products when something crazy happened. He was using his mother's blender when he put the wrong chemicals into the mix. Everything blew up, foaming up into the ceiling fan and all over his parents' kitchen walls. Initially, his parents were not happy. Then they discovered that the solution cleaned everything it touched.

The rest, they say, is history. Soon after the blender incident, Scott developed the final formula for his new cleaner—***in his mother's kitchen***. Within a few months, his company was off the ground. He chose Solv-All as the name. Why Solv-All? When his mother asked him why he was going to such lengths to invent this environmentally friendly product, Scott replied, "I'm going to **solve all** the world's problems."

When Scott began his business, financing was a huge issue. His only real options were preapproved credit card applications that he received in the mail. Every time Scott got a new form, he would apply, get the card, and max it out on some company expense. Talk about a financial plan! Today, Scott boasts that with so many credit cards, the rubber band got pretty tight.

His business plan was quite simple...he didn't have one. Scott was just trying to sell as much as he could to be able to stay afloat. Finally, his credit cards were maxed, and no one else was willing to finance him, so Scott went to the bank to apply for a loan. He was asked for a business plan, so he wrote one. He submitted his proposal; however, it was never seen again. No one even bothered to contact him or to read the plan!

My father used to ask me, "How does a mouse eat an elephant?" I would answer that it wasn't physically possible. Then, Dad would counter, "It is, if he takes one bite at a time."

Twenty years later, Solv-All is booming, taking in revenues in excess of one hundred million dollars in 2012. When asked his secret to success, Scott immediately speaks of the people he hires. He doesn't test them or absorb their résumés; he just "listens to their passion and finds out where the music is." Poetic? Yes, but extremely effective.

Think about Scott's success. It started with two things: a passionate idea and his mother's blender. With his now over twelve hundred employees, the passion is still there. Today, his mother is a happy lady...and she still has that old blender!

CHAPTER 3
Barbie Gennarelli

Founder of the Gourmet Soap
Market, LLC

Passion + Energy + Risk =
Successful Business

"I knew that I had so much energy and so many skills to put forth into something; I decided to open up a soap shop."

—Barbie Gennarelli

Barbie Gennarelli is crazy about soap. It has been a lifelong passion, her art. A successful executive with Nationwide Insurance, Barbie left her prestigious six-figure corporate job for something very different, in another universe. She opened a soap shop.

As the daughter of Slovenian immigrants, she had a dogged work ethic instilled in her at an early age. If she got an A- on a test, Barbie knew that she was to get an A or A+ on the next one. Whenever she thought that she was finished, Mom and Dad always would remind her that there was more she could do. This influence impacted her corporate career.

At Nationwide, Barbie had the distinction of being one of the first women hired to hold a largely man-held external sales position. During her tenure, Barbie became the company's top annuity sales representative and opened the door for the hiring of other women sales executives.

In return for being one of Nationwide's eighteen-year superstar performers, she was learning everything she could about the workings of a business. Barbie credits the company for teaching her business skills, from writing a quarterly business plan to creating a sales process. Those experiences created the discipline necessary to launch her start-up.

As much as she loved her coworkers and everything about Nationwide, Barbie's job demanded a lot from her. She experienced long hours, stress, and a ton of travel. She says that she does not miss all the time she spent waiting in line at airports, going from hotel to hotel, and living out of a suitcase. Corporate life was arduous.

While on the road, to alleviate stress, Barbie visited small shops in many of the cities she frequented. She enjoyed quaint little boutiques where she found new and differently crafted soaps. These visits became a great outlet for her. She not only bought from these stores, but she got to know the proprietors and cultivated relationships. Before too long, Barbie developed friendships with dozens of independent shopkeepers throughout the United States who shared her passion for unique, exhilarating, fragrant soaps.

It was time for a change. The years of being on the road took their toll. She desperately missed her family and wanted to play a bigger part in her three children's lives. She decided to turn her passion for soap into something that was part of what people do every day: take a routine shower.

"I left Nationwide to begin a new life journey. I took a huge risk, and there is no turning back now."

She wanted to take a simple shower and turn it into an experience that would make getting ready for work special.

Barbie kept thinking of all those wonderful little shops she'd visited. Then it dawned on her. She would bring together all of the fabulously crafted soaps that she'd encountered in her travels and have them made for her store. The Gourmet Soap Market was born!

The store would sell an amalgam of unique fragrant soaps for men and women. It would be the kind of place at which she would want to shop. But trying to make this dream of hers become a reality would involve a ton of risk. She had a great job and made great money. Should she throw that all away for soap? The answer was yes.

Barbie took the plunge. She made the store a reality amid the bustling downtown of Willoughby, Ohio. Sales were brisk. A spa-like atmosphere developed, with soothing music and relaxing images plus a vast array of different soap aromas.

While business was good, Barbie wasn't satisfied. People liked her establishment, but there was a lack of foot traffic. After some thought, she realized there was a serious parking issue. People had to work to get to her store. After searching for another location, she found one with adequate parking, and she bought the building. **Business doubled!**

"So when in very rare instances, something negative does come your way, I definitely try to think about their side. They are not always right, but you can make it right, and that's what I try to do."

When asked about her secret to success, Barbie references some very simple lessons she learned in her previous career. "No matter what you are selling, your focus has to be 100 percent on what the customer wants and needs."

This past year, Barbie made a customer service mistake. It would seem insignificant to 99.9 percent of the universe, but for one customer, Barbie had fallen short. One day at 4:50 p.m. she closed the store early. It was her wedding anniversary. She took a risk, locked up, and left before 5:00.

Barbie came in the next morning to find a complaint voicemail from an unhappy would-be customer who had been in a major rush to find a gift. The woman had arrived at the Gourmet Soap Company at 4:50 p.m. and found it closed. Barbie was mortified that a customer was dissatisfied, and she immediately called her back to apologize. Today, the woman is one of Barbie's best customers.

Here is what we know. In so many instances, the customer is happier with you and your company if you make a mistake and admit it. These unfortunate situations can be opportunities in disguise. The Gourmet Soap Market gets virtually no complaints except from people who may spend too much money at the store. Not a bad problem to have.

Barbie's next step is to expand into a national organization, perhaps by selling franchises in other cities. Can she do it? Don't bet against her. **If it takes energy and passion, Barbie will make it happen!**

CHAPTER 4
Tim Blankenship
Owner of Premier Dry Cleaners

Yes, Virginia, Lots of Entrepreneurs Have ADD

"We blew away our fifth year projection our second year, and the funny part about it was he and his wife became good customers over the years. Every time he'd call me, he would just smile and say, 'Boy, I sure was wrong on this one.'"

Your suit or dress that is only dry-cleanable is stained at dinner. Not a big deal, right? Just needs a trip to the drycleaner. A few days later, when you pick up the garment, the stain is gone, but the rest of the garment is ruined. You demand restitution for the damaged piece of clothing. After a heated discussion, the manager gives you a check or credit for future dry cleaning.

Meet Tim Blankenship. He started Premier Dry Cleaners over twenty years ago, and he has been at the other end of that situation. Tim agrees with you that sometimes it is the dry cleaner's fault, but more often than not, something else was responsible (e.g., the garment was made in China using uneven vegetable dyes), which precluded that piece of clothing from being safely dry-cleaned.

Tim is in the dry-cleaning business, but when it comes down to it, he is in the customer service business too. That means that he has to find ways to keep you, the customer, satisfied, even if it means cutting checks to people for ruined garments whose ruin wasn't his fault.

Tim didn't know it growing up, but he has severe attention deficit disorder that went undiagnosed until only a few years ago. No wonder he always struggled in school and was called lazy and unmotivated. Tim did receive a high school diploma, but he only lasted six weeks in college. He wasn't meant for academia, but he was equipped to be a dry cleaner.

Dry cleaning is a booming business. As it's recession-proof, Tim has found a way to increase his revenue every year of Premier's existence. Not bad for someone who barely graduated from high school.

While books weren't his passion, Tim found that he was good with his hands. At fifteen, he was hired as a delivery driver for a local dry-cleaning business. Tim became the maintenance man for the company as well. All along, he paid attention to the business and learned everything he could about dry cleaning. Not surprisingly, Tim was quickly promoted to the production manager position.

With his dry-cleaning experience, Tim decided to take the next step. He wanted his own business. It was natural and made sense; however, like so many other entrepreneurs, his biggest roadblock was money. He had none!

"But I kept asking…Why am I getting turned down?"

Tim recalls dealing with a family friend named Bill when he was trying to secure his business loan through a local bank. Bill was a big-hearted guy who wanted to help him out. He gave Tim advice on his business plan and suggested names for the new company. Tim took the next step and asked Bill to invest some money for start-up capital, but unfortunately, Bill had to turn him down. Bill wasn't convinced that Tim would be able to get the market share he had outlined in the business plan.

Next, Tim tried to secure a bank loan; he applied to several large and small banks, but he kept getting rejected. Tim estimates that he was denied over twenty times by ten different banks. After his third attempt at one bank, Tim finally got his loan. Tim was thrilled because now he could start his company.

At the end of his second year in business, Premier Dry Cleaners obliterated its revenue and market share projections *for year five!* Oddly enough, his old friend Bill had become a regular client of Premier. Every time Bill dropped off his laundry, he would smile and say, "Boy, I sure was wrong on this one!"

Tim understands the business and has a passion for dry cleaning. A workaholic, he will put in an eighty-hour workweek between his two locations, like many other successful entrepreneurs. Tim gets so lost in his work; his wife will often call and remind him to come home for dinner.

Tim Blankenship is a prime example of how you don't have to keep a Harvard 4.0 grade point average to be a successful entrepreneur. The secret to his success is simple. Tim is passionate about what he does. It shows in the way he treats his staff and his customers.

The secret to Tim's success is simple. He has a passion for dry cleaning, and it manifests itself in how he treats his staff, how he serves his customers, and how hard he works.

CHAPTER 5
John Allin

Founder of Snow
Management Group and
Snow Dragon Snowmelters

*It All Started with
One Snowplow*

"Like most people who start out, I had nothing. I didn't even dream of being a very large company. I was trying to make a little extra money on the side. I was a salesman. I sold welding equipment, and I took my Christmas bonus and bought my first plow."

—JOHN ALLIN

John Allin is a man of contrasts. When presented with an opportunity to work in the snow and ice management field, he took it and ran. Then, when given another possibility, what looked to be a once in a lifetime chance, John had the patience and wisdom to turn the option down. He was dead right with his instincts and business sense in both instances. Three multi-million-dollar companies (and more than one patent) are the result of his superior business intuition.

Let's move backward a few years. John sold welding equipment for a living. It paid the bills, but he found himself wanting to make a little bit more, just to cover a few extra expenses. So one December day back in the late 1970s, John took his Christmas bonus and bought a snowplow to attach to a Ford Bronco. He lived in Erie, Pennsylvania, so he was pretty confident he would find work. (Erie gets over twelve feet of snow in any given year.) This new venture started out simply enough; however, by 2004, John owned the largest snow removal company in North America.

How did he do it? John admits that things started out slowly. He began plowing snow like most snow contractors, just removing snow on driveways and commercial sites in Erie. John learned to manage the process and developed a system. Next, he found other snow removal entrepreneurs and expanded his business through subcontracting. He simply taught the subcontractors what he wanted them to do and assigned the work. By the late 1990s, John had secured a contract with Wachovia Bank that granted his company thirteen hundred snow removal sites. Then, opportunity *really* knocked.

In late 2000, word spread within the industry that the Salt Lake City Winter Olympics was going to subcontract all of its snow removal for its games. John's name was just one on an extraordinarily long list to bid for the business. Fortunately, he was selected to submit a bid.

John went through the process and was told that the Olympic committee had awarded the business to some local companies in Utah.

But there was some tertiary business for smaller work that was still being bid on, and John was asked to submit another proposal. Now, however, they wanted him to do several bids with different pricing based upon how much risk the Salt Lake City Games was willing to take with the snow removal work. John decided to really get their attention and simply offered to do one work for the four smaller sites for one flat fee, assuming all of the risk in case the snowfall was light.

He had their attention. At that point, the Salt Lake City Games were badly over budget, and the higher-ups were sweating bullets about paying massive amounts of money for snow removal that might not even be necessary or needed. The fact that John Allin was willing to take the risk in this situation moved him right up to the front of the line for this contract. Then he pulled the old "Columbo" close, and as he was leaving the meeting, he said, "Oh, by the way, I can do the whole project for a flat fee of four and a half million dollars." The phone rang shortly after he got to the airport to go back to Erie. The Games wanted him to come back to talk...***now***. John cancelled his flight back to Erie and went back and inked a deal to do all the snow removal for the Olympics for a flat fee of just under five million dollars.

> *"You don't want to jump at every little thing to come down the pipe either. You want to make sure you pick and choose and everybody gets the attention that they deserve."* —*John Allin*

This became the high profile job that really put John on the map. Soon he was getting phone calls for business from all over the place. Right in the middle of the Salt Lake City Olympics job, he was contacted by CVS (a national pharmacy chain), wanting him to contract to manage the snow services at over twenty-six hundred sites.

Quite the opportunity...one would think. Believe it or not, John turned the offer down. Everyone was telling him that if he didn't jump all over this opportunity, he wasn't going to get another chance. John stood by his guns and walked away. It wasn't the right timing. He already was swamped with the Olympics. One year later, his newfound reputation preceding him, CVS called again, and John accepted the contract.

The Olympics proved to be the springboard for his success, but it was also the genesis for a new product that would turn the snow removal industry on its ear. One of the many problems John faced when he went to tackle the Olympics job was what to do with the plowed snow rather than haul it off-site. Then, after his company had been awarded the contract, the Olympic committee mandated that because of 9/11, which had happened just six months before the games, all the snow had to be hauled off every site for security reasons. There could be no piles higher than eighteen inches. It wasn't an easy task; however, John honored the committee's request (for an additional fee, of course).

"They put me in touch with the parent company that fell in love with the idea and said, 'you're not going to find someone else to build this. We can do it for you. Oh, and by the way, you'd better sell your company because we want you to come and work for us.'" —John Allin

John knew that off-site snow removal wasn't the answer for most businesses. There were no portable melt devices available to get rid of the snow at the time. So after the Olympics, he sat down and engineered a piece of equipment that solved the problem. Snow and ice would be put onto a melting pan immersed in a hot water bath containing heat exchanger tubes. The burner would fire into the tubes, heating the water. As snow would be dumped onto the hot water bath, warm water would be sprayed over it. As the snow melted, it would travel down the pan, through a screening process into the debris catch area, and back into the water hopper to be reheated. John's new idea was mobile and eco-friendly and it melted snow truckloads at a time. He was on to something.

After making phone calls and speaking with contacts, John found a company that would help him engineer his new pet project. As chance would have it, the company was part of a larger corporation, which got wind of the project and fell in love with his idea. The parent corporation convinced him to sell his stake in the Snow Management Group (the same business he'd founded and nurtured from nothing to industry dominance). They ended up financing the start-up company that John would name The Snow Dragon. Today, Snow Dragons are sold all over the world—even in Moscow, Russia, which became Snow Dragon's biggest customer.

It all started with a Ford Bronco and one snowplow.

CHAPTER 6
Angela Timperio
Founder and CEO of
Life Safety Enterprises

"What me? Marry and have ten kids? Not going to happen!"

"The better I make you look, the better I look."

—ANGELA TIMPERIO

Ten-year-old girls are adorable. Little Angela Timperio was that little cute ten-year-old who not only played with dolls but loved to play business...literally. When the other girls had tea parties and sleepovers, little Angela was pretending to be the CEO of a company. That's right! Dolls were fine, but Angela always knew that she was destined to become a businesswoman.

As she was growing up, Angela's father had his own small business. He owned and operated a barbershop. Every day, Angela would go directly from school to Dad's work. There she was to sit and complete all of her homework before they went home for dinner. As she studied, Angela listened to the conversations her dad had with his customers. She loved the way he interacted with everyone and how he conducted his business. She kept thinking to herself how incredible it would be to have her own company.

Like so many entrepreneurs, Angela's journey to own and manage her own business was unique. Angela is an Italian-American. She grew up with parents who wanted her to adhere to the family's strict Italian roots. This meant that Angela was to skip college, get married young, have ten children, and spend her life as a homemaker. Angela did marry and have a daughter, but she had no intention of being a stay at home mom for the rest of her life.

With no college degree, Angela managed to secure an entry-level job in sales and marketing with a local company called Ecocenters, where her extraordinary passion and drive made her successful as she quickly rose to be vice president of sales and marketing. Angela was darn good at her job and had no need for a college degree if she was going to stay at Ecocenters. But realizing that not having a degree could limit future opportunities, Angela enrolled in college and completed her undergraduate work while working for Ecocenters. It took Angela seven and a half years to earn her diploma.

Time went by, and Angela was a success. She was able to exhale for a brief moment after receiving her bachelor's degree, but she wanted to become an entrepreneur. In 1998, while still at Ecocenters, Angela started her own marketing agency called Mosaic Marketing. Mosaic was her initial attempt to fulfill her dream, but it was only the beginning of her entrepreneurial journey.

"When a lot of little girls were playing dolls, at age ten, I was playing businesswoman."

Within a few months, Angela had acquired a small base of clients. Among them was a firefighter who had a side business doing safety inspections and training. Specifically, this was a tiny company with two part-time employees and less than fifty thousand dollars a year in billable business. The fireman hadn't put much time into the company and wasn't sure about the direction of the organization. In their conversations, he and Angela came to two conclusions: he knew life safety, and Angela knew marketing. So they became partners.

Angela left Ecocenters and devoted all of her time to their new venture. She had some knowledge of life safety, since both her husband and father-in-law were firefighters. Within a short time frame, Angela was able to come up with a long-term vision for the company. It would move in three different directions. First, it would provide training services to hospitals, and then it would continue inspections for fire and general safety to satisfy OSHA requirements. Finally, it would move to offer remediation and repairs to companies in violation of OSHA standards.

Off they went. Angela's passion for learning life safety and for the business grew and grew. Her partner wasn't as enthusiastic, so within a few months, Angela arranged to buy out his stock in Life Safety Enterprises.

Life Safety was unique. Angela, the new sole owner, immersed herself in learning and staying current with safety issues. She became the **brand** of Life Safety Enterprises.

Today, the company has grown by leaps and bounds. When you need to have your staff trained in any number of safety issues, you call Life Safety Enterprises. When you have an OSHA violation, you call Life Safety to help you fix the problem. When you want to avoid having OSHA come down hard on you, you call Angela's company to get the expertise needed for violation-free inspections. Her employees know safety front, back, and sideways. They are the experts.

At this writing, Angela employs over twenty-five people in Ohio and Florida. She is in the process of adding certifications that will allow her to do business in more states. Recently, Angela has moved out of the day-to-day operations of the company. With the daily business on autopilot, she spends her time "on her business, not in it."

Today there are twenty-five employees and lots of organizations that are very glad Angela didn't stay home and have ten children. Developing a viable business and finding opportunities that no one else saw was in her DNA. It's her **secret to success**.

CHAPTER 7
Fahim Gemayel
Founder of Lakeland
Management Systems

Coming to America

"I started Lakeland Management Systems out of a phone booth, out of a pay phone at a BP station. I had no desk, knew little English, and had no know-how."

—FAHIM GEMAYEL

Fahim's story is not unlike those of many people who come to the United States. He came looking for opportunity, and through sweat and smarts, he was able to create value. Growing up in Lebanon certainly wasn't easy. It is a nation that has been torn apart by wars and terrorism for the past forty years.

When he was younger, Fahim experienced firsthand the anguish and sorrow that wars and political strife produce. His cousin, President Elect Bashir Gemayel, was assassinated. So the United States was an opportunity for him to escape the war, finish his education, and try his hand at the American way. Many years later, he has become a poster child for the American Dream.

Fresh out of Case Western Reserve University and Lake Erie College, Fahim set out to make his way. In June of 1986, Lakeland Management Systems, a multi-million-dollar a year construction company in northeast Ohio, was born. The challenges that Fahim faced trying to get a fledgling company off the ground included a lack of financing, an inability to find customers, and not being able to find good employees. Besides these challenges, Fahim struggled with the English language.

He had a background in engineering from his studies at Case Western Reserve University, but he was very uncertain of how the building contracting industry worked in the United States. On a radio show, Fahim smiled and admitted that he had no clue how to begin structuring his business.

Despite many uncertainties, an extraordinarily limited grasp of the English language, and a lack of understanding about his new country and chosen professional field, Fahim moved forward and set up shop with Lakeland Management Systems in a phone booth on Route 91 in Orange, Ohio, on June 24, 1986.

"I saw a need for change. I saw an opportunity. I saw a need of challenge. I saw a need of success. I found them in this country, and they all exist, and they are real. So the hungers that drive, the opportunity, the challenge, made me a better person and made me see what this country is all about."

Fahim had a strong work ethic and a vision of what he wanted Lakeland Management Systems to be. While he knew that he was basically starting off with nothing, with the possible exception of the phone booth, Fahim had a positive attitude. America, land of opportunity, motivated him to take a huge business risk. Currently, his business does projects for the following Fortune 500 companies: Pepsi-Cola, Subway, McDonald's, Eaton Corporation, and Avery Denison. Wow!

As with most entrepreneurial ventures, nothing immediately fell into place for Lakeland Management Systems. There were tough times

> *"Everybody thinks that the grass is greener on the other side. Let's go ahead and open up, get a desk, get a phone, put ads in the paper, and the phone will start ringing. It doesn't work like that today. And I found out the hard way. Not all of the twenty-four years in this business have been a great ride. It has had its ups and downs."*

early on. With absolutely no training in managing a company, Fahim had to learn virtually everything about operating a business while he was running the daily operation. Managing employees, dealing with banks and architects, and promoting efficient customer service were all skills that he worked to master along the way.

Small-business owners and entrepreneurs cringe when they get that knock on the door or that phone call at 5:00 p.m. on Friday evening when they are hoping to sneak out for a dinner with the family or to catch their child's baseball game. The caller says, "There is a customer problem with…" After a few expletives and a two-hour emergency meeting, the issue gets solved…or at least controlled. Ever the optimist, Fahim sees these business challenges in a different light than so many of his peers do. He embraces them, because to Fahim, they are signs of relevance, reassurances that his company is a player in the industry.

> *"When you're in business, if you don't have everyday challenge(s) that means you don't have a business, because nobody cares about your business."*

Another important factor that leads to the success of Fahim Gemayel as a businessman is his reputation. He always says, "I have one thing: my name." Keeping his reputation and his name clean has always been on top of Fahim's priorities list. The trust he has built among his clients, employees, and suppliers is unshakable.

Fahim Gemayel: Living the American dream!

CHAPTER 8
Jason Kintzler
Founder of Pitch Engine

When It's Meant to Be,
It Will Happen.

"When I quit the news business, my family thought I was crazy."

—JASON KINTZLER

Jason Kintzler was born and raised in Landor, Wyoming. He attended college at Montana State University as a rugby athlete and then returned home to Landor. Jason loved Wyoming's scenery, landscape, and people. There are only seven hundred thousand people in the state, and seven thousand are residents of Landor. It is a great place to raise children, and yes…a great place to start a business.

Jason began as a local TV newscaster and then worked at a media branding company. It might have been the Wyoming wind, but something inside told him that the press release and branding industry had to change. He saw that there was a better way to perform the all-important press release function and distribute these releases to millions of people without the high cost from the major PR firms.

Jason had one small problem. He didn't have any start-up capital. In fact, he had no money at all. So many entrepreneurs begin with no capital and find a way to succeed. Jason did too, but it wasn't a cakewalk. However, his new wife, Jasmine, was very supportive. She constantly said, "When it's meant to be, it will happen."

In his early thirties, Jason wanted to start his press release dream company. He already knew its name—**Pitch Engine**. It was to be the first public platform built for a new kind of storyteller: his clients. It would be brand-based and would travel the Internet. His customers could upload photos, videos, and podcasts and could write their own text.

> *His new wife, Jasmine, was very supportive. She constantly said, "When it's meant to be, it will happen."*

The press release would be for everyone to see, not just journalists. It would cost a fraction of what the big companies charged. One click, and the press release, shared via e-mail and all the social media outlets, including Facebook, Twitter, and LinkedIn, could be seen by the world.

Jason needed ten thousand dollars to start **Pitch Engine**. He also had to hire a programmer before the company could be launched. Jason didn't have the skill to do the high-tech work. Enter fate!

While working for another company, Jason was with his wife at a convention in Las Vegas. On a lark, he decided to play the penny slots. Suddenly, Jason hit the jackpot and won thirty-six hundred dollars. It wasn't the ten thousand dollars that he needed, but it was a good start. The thirty-six hundred dollars was his "meant to be moment."

Jason didn't waste much time. From the casino, he called a programmer and hired him over the phone. **Pitch Engine** officially started. Jason's dream was going to come true.

We have seen all kinds of ways to fund a company. Many entrepreneurs obtain equity lines of credit on their homes. Some get funding from the "three Fs," fools, friends, and family. Others even obtain start-up capital from crowd funding sites and angel investors. But raising money through gambling? It just doesn't happen. Call it luck, or destiny, or the effect of the Wyoming wind. The cash prize winnings worked for Jason!

Founded in 2009, Pitch Engine by the end of 2012 had over forty thousand clients, or brands, as Jason calls them. His company growth is staggering, and his platform has been called one of the PR industry's most transformative innovations. Jason says, "It isn't just a website or piece of software; it's a new way of doing business."

Jason is first to admit that this is only the beginning. He understands that what has been created is something people don't know they need. He also points out that when Henry Ford, founder of Ford Motor, asked people what they needed, they said *faster horses*!

Pitch Engine has been such a success that many suitors have come through Jason's door. He's been offered piles of cash and has even had venture capitalists offer to help him fund the company. Jason turned them all down. Does this surprise you, from a guy that started his company by winning at the penny slots? No, it probably doesn't.

When asked his secrets to success, he offered three things:

1. Be grounded and authentic as a person. Know who you are.

2. Be different. Think outside the box and innovate. Challenge the status quo and find new solutions to old problems.

3. Work hard!

We haven't heard the last of Jason Kintzler. He will continue to innovate, give his best effort, and thrive. Put your sunglasses on; Jason Kintzler's future is very bright!

CHAPTER 9
Ray Kralovic
Co-Founder of STERIS

Thrown into the Pool

"I was standing near the edge and somebody pushed me in. I had the best time because I was first, splashing all of the other kids. Then I pulled them into the pool with me. That reminds me of how I got pushed into becoming an entrepreneur."

Ray Kralovic didn't exactly want to become an entrepreneur. If you ask him, he will tell you he was pretty much dragged into it kicking and screaming. It was the mid-1980s, and this West Virginia man had a good job working for AMSCO, the largest manufacturer of sterilization equipment in the country. He was married and had four children. He had a good life.

The problem was that Ray is smart...very smart. He watched and listened, using his background, a PhD in Microbiology, to figure out a solution to a problem the medical world had been facing for its entire existence: the sterilization of instruments. His idea would revolutionize how hospitals sanitized their instruments, improving the lives of countless surgery patients and at the same time making AMSCO a boatload of money. You would think Ray would have been a hero to the powers that be in the company. But oddly enough, his invention got him fired.

Ray had this idea floating around in the back of his mind for some time. The state of technology in the world of surgery during the 1980s was limited. There were certain surgical instruments that could not stand up to the steam sterilization processes of the day.

It was regular practice during this period for hospitals to have these outcast instruments undergo a disinfecting process instead.

While the instruments would be reusable, they were not in fact sterile (100 percent free of microbes), and they posed a greater infection risk than the sterilized instruments. Hospitals faced the dilemma of how to disinfect colonoscopes with a solution after each surgical procedure. Ray's process simply allowed for all of these instruments to be sterilized.

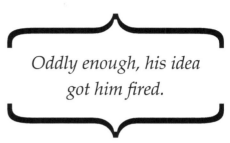

Oddly enough, his idea got him fired.

Dr. Kralovic knew that he had something with his sterilization idea. It just made sense. He started pushing the idea to AMSCO. He promoted his idea to anyone at the company who would listen to him. The problem was that the development directors at AMSCO weren't interested. Ray kept going. Despite refusal after refusal after refusal, Ray continued to press the Research and Development Department for funding. Nothing happened.

As is typical of large companies, AMSCO didn't want to rock the boat. The executives liked their market share and excellent profits. In their view, there was no real reason to jump in on this new idea. The proposal was too revolutionary, too radical, and definitely too risky.

On July 4, 1985, the families of the employees at AMSCO were gathered for a company picnic. Ray decided to use the occasion to ask for funding yet another time. His attempt to get management to listen to him failed again, and Ray was fired on the spot.

Not without resources, Ray was able to find a professorship position at Case Western Reserve University in Cleveland, Ohio. This was both good and bad news. The good part was that he would have access to the University's lab facilities to embark on the testing process for his sterilization brainchild. The bad part was that he lived just west of Erie, Pennsylvania, and his family had absolutely no interest in moving.

For weeks, Ray would make a daily one hundred-sixty-mile commute from Erie to Cleveland. He taught classes and did research for fourteen hours a day. It was grueling, but Ray was as focused as a laser beam.

Ray and his engineer friend and business partner Ed Schneider started making phone calls. They needed capital…badly. Eventually they were able to talk to a couple of venture capital companies in Cleveland. A company called Primus Venture Capital (in addition to what Ray calls friends, fools, and family) agreed to provide some start-up funding. All in all, he and his partner raised about $120,000. Quite a sum in the 1980s, but it just didn't appear to be enough for what they wanted to do. Still, they forged ahead.

By the end of 1985, Ray developed what would become the first liquid sterilization system on the world market. Having named it System One, he started filing for his first patents. By 1988, he finalized and patented the liquid sterilization solution for use in the System One processor. Late in the year, Ray and his investors brought in professional executive help and shipped their first units. From then on, they didn't look back. The company, Steris, started growing by leaps and bounds.

Today Steris is a giant in the medical industry. It is a multi-billion-dollar a year company that employs over five thousand people and has offices in sixty countries. Steris continues to push the envelope of medical and surgical innovation around the world.

In 1996, Steris succeeded in acquiring AMSCO, a premier manufacturer and global supplier of sterilization systems. Yes, AMSCO the same company that had unceremoniously dismissed Ray at the company picnic eleven years earlier. A devastating blow created a new technology and a renowned company.

Dr. Ray Kralovic: Survivor. Inventor. Entrepreneur.

> Ray Kralovic's secret to success is his persistence and patience in working tirelessly to develop a product. This reluctant entrepreneur now is the epitome of the successful businessman. He just wouldn't give up!

CHAPTER 10
Cathy Horton, Esq.
Founder of Nutek
& Renegade Brands

Find That Point of Pain

"Talk to your customers and find their point of pain. It's not about the point of purchase; it's about what's their point of pain — because there isn't going to be any point of purchase if there is no point of pain that you're solving."

—Cathy Horton

Have you ever been introduced to or met someone who, after a brief minute of conversation, you could tell was a successful person?

If your answer is no, then chances are, you haven't met Cathy Horton.

Cathy founded Nutek, a company that developed and marketed a line of fourteen green retail products and forty-four industrial products (including lubricants and cleaners), in 2007. She doesn't shy away from challenges, as evidenced by the number of hats Cathy has worn in her career: entrepreneur, attorney, Episcopal priest... all of which she attacks with an incredible amount of drive, focus, energy, and enthusiasm.

Rewind ten years. Cathy is a practicing mergers and acquisitions attorney who is transplanted to the United Kingdom to work for the Cabinet Office of Prime Minister Tony Blair. Her previous experience working as an attorney for companies on the NASDAQ exchange gave her plenty of exposure to all sorts of new breakthroughs. So much so that Cathy set up a consulting company in

Britain focusing on technology solutions, economic development, how to take technologies and transform economies, and how to create economic clusters from technologies.

After her tour abroad, Cathy returned to the United States and went back to her law practice. In addition, she set up another consulting company that focused on commercializing technologies. One of the technologies was seeking a WD-40 equivalent. Yes, WD-40, the multi-use lubricant. Yes, WD-40, the same lubrication product that has had the lion's share of the market for the past fifty years. Product after product after product has tried to challenge it over the years, all of them quickly knocked out by this multi-use lubrication heavyweight. Cathy researched this product, even going to the WD-40 headquarters to speak with CEO Gary Ridge.

Unimpressed with the product and what it did, she started moving forward as a competitor to this giant organization.

At this point, Cathy had to deal with two minor hurdles. She still didn't have a product to sell or a retailer to get the product that she didn't have to the customers. No big deal, right? She took a chance and e-mailed and then

"And so, we contacted the lead buyer at Home Depot and went down and said, look, are you interested in the Green Lubricant line? If you are, what do you think of these ideas? What do you think of this can? What do you think of this nozzle? What do you think of these brands? What do you think of these product claims? If you had a product, what would you want it to do?"

called up the head of hardware purchasing at Home Depot. At the time, Home Depot carried a lot of top of the line lubricant products (WD-40 among them).

Then Cathy started asking a lot of questions. Why? She was trying to find a way to ease the buyer's company's points of pain, which are problems, challenges, voids, and issues that we all have to deal with on a daily basis. Because consumers buy based on emotional pain, if you can find a way to ease your prospective customer's points of pain, you have created something of value that can be marketed.

"They were invested in us, us in them, and the co-created, the co-thinking, shared philosophy, the passion around the products, all of a sudden, you have a customer that's your partner."

The buyer at Home Depot spoke candidly with her about what he liked and didn't like and about problems with the line of products that his company carried. Cathy listened and investigated further into what Home Depot really wanted and needed. Then she went to work with her team, creating and designing a product that would ease both Home Depot's and the future customer's pain.

For two years Cathy went back to the buyer over and over again, asking more questions, testing, refining, and making sure that her product would in fact compete with WD-40. From these Home Depot conversations, Cathy was able to gain a customer that was also Nutek's partner.

The result of **Nutek's** listening, collaborating, and innovating was the christening of three new green lubricants: Lubfix®, Bolt Off®, and Shield It®. Lubfix® gets rid of creaks and squeaks. Bolt Off® loosens stuck nuts and bolts. Shield It® prevents rust. All three products outperformed WD-40 in independent testing. Today, they are major players in the lubricant market, challenging WD-40, the leader in the retail and industrial marketplace.

After a year of development, Home Depot began carrying **Nutek's** green lubricants in its stores across the country. Not long after, other big retailers fell into line. True Value, Northern Tool, Tractor Supply, Ace Hardware, Auto Zone, and Kroger all signed on. By 2009, Nutek had attracted the interest of Hoover, who then decided to buy the company.

Recently, Cathy left Hoover. She has started her seventh company, **Renegade Brands,** which features two new products, Gas Off® wipes and Sweat X Sports Laundry Detergent®. Both address the customer's point of pain. That's Cathy, the super entrepreneur! What will she find next?

> "I don't like to be told something is impossible. I think if you want something and you want to achieve something and you believe in something, you can absolutely do it. "

CHAPTER 11
Diana Richards
Founder of Vacuum Systems International

From Near Homeless to Successful Entrepreneur

"I was asking the universe, 'Where am I supposed to be?' and the universe said, 'OK, you're supposed to be starting a vacuum cleaner company.'"

—DIANA RICHARDS

Diana Richards was in a rut. Recently divorced, her children in college or out on their own, she took a job working as an operations manager for a vacuum cleaner company in Cleveland, Ohio. It was a good job, and she was a respected employee. Diana's twenty years' experience in the vacuum cleaner industry was pleasant enough, but something was missing.

With no intention of picking up stakes from her home in New Castle, Pennsylvania, Diana would drive into Cleveland on Monday nights and drive home on Saturday afternoons. During these drives, she would do a lot of thinking about her situation, realizing that something had to change.

Enter fate. One morning, the phone rang. The lady on the other end of the line had a strange request. Her name was Kristin, and she was a manager of a retail chain of clothing

"Diana, we need you. The retail industry needs you."

stores. She was assigned the task of purchasing and maintaining all of the chain's vacuum cleaners. This was an undertaking that Kristin knew absolutely nothing about, and she needed help badly.

She asked Diana's professional advice about vacuum cleaner purchases and repairs.

Diana obliged and put together a seminar on everything she had learned in her twenty years of experience. After the meeting, Kristin looked at her and said, "Diana, we need you. The retail industry needs you. There is no one out there telling us how to buy vacuum cleaners and maintain vacuum cleaners in our stores. I bet you'd be a millionaire if you taught us how to do that."

Then Diana asked Kristin the million-dollar question, the question so many successful business people ask of their prospective clients: "What do you need?" Kristin replied, "An 800 number that we could call for an immediate vacuum advice and repair."

Elated, Diana ran out to her car and wrote the word "Helpline" on the top of a yellow legal pad. She wrote down everything that Kristin talked about. Finally, Diana organized a simple process that could be used to service the vacuums.

Everything seemed in place for this venture to begin. Kristin seemed as excited about this idea as Diana. The two started calling each other at their homes to talk. Kristin was intelligent about technology and had an MBA. She helped Diana write a business plan.

Everything was in place to get this company off the ground—**everything but money**. Without it, Diana's big idea would remain a dream. Diana knew one thing for certain: no bank in its right mind was going to give a divorced fifty-year-old with little collateral, no customers, and no business a loan.

When Diana first started spending time in Cleveland, looking for a way to meet people in her new town, she placed a personal ad in a local newspaper. Through her advertisement, she met a businessman with lots of experience. They never wound up dating, but they did talk a lot about business. He made the offhand comment that Diana needed to have her own company. He suggested that if she ever came up with a viable business idea, he wanted to know.

Diana did call him, and they met. She presented her idea, and the first thing he did was to try to talk her out of it. He reminded Diana that her friends and family were going to think

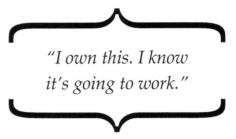

"I own this. I know it's going to work."

that she was nuts. For the better part of an hour, he basically said, "It might work. Has this ever been done before?" Diana was persistent. She said, "No it's never been done before, but I own this. I know it's going to work. I have seen the broken vacuums. I have talked to the stores. I know this is going to work." They spent four more hours in a conference room talking about the idea. He started to whiteboard it. Finally, he said, "OK, I'll fund it for you."

Diana was taken aback. She went to talk to this man to get some ideas, some feedback on her thoughts. She'd had no idea that she was pitching her company to an investor. He said that he would fund her company up

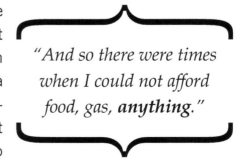

*"And so there were times when I could not afford food, gas, **anything**."*

to twenty-five thousand dollars. In return, he would be her silent partner, a fifty/fifty split. But there was a caveat. He insisted that she quit her day job and then locate the company headquarters/warehouse on his street in Mentor, Ohio, so that he could watch the operation. She jumped at the opportunity. He walked her across the hall of his building to an attorney's office and got her company legally incorporated. Her company was born.

Diana didn't quit her job. She worked out a plan with her boss to work part-time. Then she found a warehouse in which to start up. She borrowed a card table and some folding chairs and purchased a telephone and a fax machine. She called up Kristen and said, "I have a business, and I need a customer." Together they went and sat down with Kristen's bosses. She worked at a big company; they had over three hundred stores. Diana and Kristin pitched Vacuum Systems International and walked out the door with her first customer.

The twenty-five thousand dollars was going quickly. The system Diana had put in place to fix the vacuums was working, but **she** was the one fixing them. Spending virtually 100 percent of her time as a technician and not as a CEO was hurting her business. Her partner walked in the door one day and gave her an ultimatum. With money running low, he reminded her that he was only in for twenty-five thousand dollars. Diana needed to find more business. That meant hiring a technician, with her hitting the streets to find more clients. However, she didn't have the capital for a technician. She did own a house, though. With that house as collateral, Diana secured a loan for thirty-five thousand dollars so she could hire a technician and go out and sell her idea.

Having friends is important. Diana had sunk everything she had into Vacuum Systems International. Friends would slip her twenty dollars here and there because she had no money for gas. Eateries at the strip mall next door to the warehouse would drop food off at her door. Living at her warehouse, she would go over to the local Bally's to work out and shower and get ready for her days. There were times when she could not afford **anything**.

What kept her going? Diana turned on the positive thinking tapes and moved forward. She visualized, meditated, and **kept her eye on the prize**. She could see it so clearly. There were the technicians lined up doing the work. She envisioned the vacuum cleaners. The trucks were coming in with broken units and leaving with them fixed. ***Her vision was clear. It was going to happen.***

It did happen. Diana started flying to corporate headquarters all over the country to sell her idea. In June of 1996 (one year from the company's inception), Vacuum Systems International signed a big customer. In September, she signed another big customer. Diana found that once she showed the operations managers how much easier her company could make their lives, new clients came on regularly. In the company's first year, Diana brought in four hundred thousand dollars in business.

To date, Vacuum Systems International has grossed millions. Just through listening and asking what was needed, this virtually homeless fifty-year-old divorcée created not just a product but an entire industry. Diana isn't homeless anymore. In fact, she has several homes scattered around the United States. With good use of today's technology and with the operations portion of Vacuum Systems International on auto pilot, she visits all of them frequently.

Diana's secret to success was keeping a positive attitude. Even in the bad times, that attitude made the difference between success and failure.

CHAPTER 12
Tierra Destiny Reid
Founder of Stylish Designs

"Being laid off was the door that opened wide."

"I never thought I would thank God for my pink slip. It was my passage to finding my purpose."

— TIERRA DESTINY REID

This military wife and mother of two children had a good job at a large national department store doing what she loved, but while on maternity leave, she found out (on CNN!) that her entire department was closing. Tierra Destiny Reid was now a new mother, and she had no job. To make matters worse, she found out about losing her job while watching cable news.

Tierra has often said that being laid off was "the door that opened wide." She was now even more determined to succeed. A new goal was to become an entrepreneur. Tierra knew it was **now or never**.

Early in her life, she was continually starting businesses. Selling candy and even starting a babysitting club were her first ventures. While in college at the University of Georgia, Tierra started a gift basket company in her dorm room. She sold the baskets to college men who wanted unique gifts for their girlfriends.

From her small-business experience, Tierra began understanding costs, the art of negotiation, salesmanship, and time management. Yet she still needed to learn more about entrepreneurship to be successful. Tierra went back to the University of Georgia and reconnected with Chris Hanks, the director of entrepreneurship. They talked not about how to start a business but which business to start first. Then she talked with other entrepreneurs and learned their language and secrets of success.

Scared or not, Tierra took the plunge and opened Stylish Consignments. She designed her company to inspire and assist women in living their best lives by making good shopping choices, at discounted prices, in an upscale store. Customers generated an extra stream of income by selling their gently worn clothes. It worked. Her company is thriving and very profitable, and Tierra is considered one of the most admired entrepreneurs in the Atlanta area.

Tierra had heard horror stories about entrepreneurs over- borrowing and overspending to start their companies and then going broke. That wasn't going to happen to her. She didn't want to go into debt, so her start-up cash came from the severance package received from her layoff. Then Tierra really got frugal.

All the Stylish Consignment's fixtures and decorations were bought used. She got her decorations inventory from a failed boutique near Atlanta and from family and friends. Her fixtures came from Craigslist. She bought three thousand dollars' worth of fixtures for five hundred dollars, and then she sold

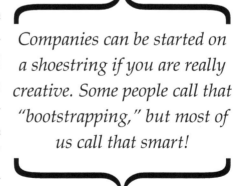

Companies can be started on a shoestring if you are really creative. Some people call that "bootstrapping," but most of us call that smart!

what she didn't need and recouped her investment. All her fixtures ended up being free. Now that's a good businesswoman!

As with most entrepreneurs, when first starting a business, Tierra's emotions ran high. During her soft opening, her initial customer was the manager of another consignment store. The woman bought a pair of shoes. Tierra was so nervous she forgot how to use the credit card machine. The customer finally paid in cash. Instead of keeping the money, Tierra had the customer sign the bills. They were framed and hung on the wall as a memento of her first sale. As Tierra says, some things are meant to be.

Tierra is so successful that she has been featured on many Atlanta cable television shows, including ABC, CBS, and FOX. She has also had an article written about her in the Atlanta Constitution and has been interviewed on a variety of business radio shows.

Now Tierra is reciprocating. She spends a lot of her time coaching and advising other women entrepreneurs. Tierra plans and schedules many start-up events across the country. She counsels other would-be entrepreneurs to start something different.

Tierra often says, "Doing what everyone else is doing will get you what everyone else has. Listen to your inner spirit and follow your dreams." When asked if everyone can be an entrepreneur, Tierra emphatically says *no*! Entrepreneurs cannot be afraid of failure, and most people are.

Tierra is proud of what she's accomplished. When her layoff was announced on CNN, it was a catalyst for her future success. As she said, "I never thought I would thank God for my pink slip. It was my passage to finding my purpose."

Tierra Destiny Reid: Entrepreneur. Role model. Teacher.

CHAPTER 13
Keith Schroeder
Founder of High Road Craft Ice Cream & Sorbet

It Just Took One Phone Call

And so a bunch of guys came by casually dressed, tasted the product, and said, "Oh we have to have these in our stores.'"

—KEITH SCHROEDER

The restaurant business is tough. Elite chefs like Keith Schroeder have to be alert, resourceful, and motivated to be successful. For example, you are running the kitchen at a high-end café at an airport, and one of the flights has a long delay. All of sudden, you have to figure out how to feed two hundred people in a half hour. Keith is the guy who could pull that nightmare off and have the patrons hoping that their flight gets held up the next time they're in town.

In addition to spending time as an executive chef at the New England Culinary Institute, for twenty years Keith was the top chef in renowned restaurants in New York, San Diego, and Los Angeles. He knew all the ice cream products on the market.

Keith, like so many chefs, was not without his preferences and biases. He had strong opinions about what ice cream should and shouldn't be. When planning events as a chef, Keith was often asked to put ice cream on the menu. The problem was that none of the retail ice creams really impressed him. Even as an accomplished chef, Keith really wasn't in a position where he could call up Häagen-Dazs or Ben and Jerry's and ask them to generate flavors he thought would be fast sellers. It just wasn't going to happen.

Keith thought about adding different fruits to recipes. Also, there was a specific type of chocolate he loved that wasn't found in commercial ice cream. So Keith started making his own ice cream to serve at the special events his hotels catered. He started filling what he deemed to be a giant hole in the business-to-business ice cream market.

The process was a rather quick one. He did his due diligence and spoke with other chefs around the area. He was able to get commitments from a good portion of them. It was decided that if Keith produced this premium ice cream, they would buy from him and use the upscale ice cream on their menus. So began the idea for High Road Craft Ice Cream & Sorbet, not as a retail operation, like so many ice cream companies before it, but as a supplier to other professional kitchens.

The best way Keith could think of to continue his ice cream operation was to go back to school and learn about business. He enrolled at Kennesaw State University. For his Cornerstone project, Keith was asked to create a business plan for some product or service.

He persuaded his team to use his ice cream idea for their product. The plan was excellent...beyond excellent, so much so that his professor took note and enrolled the group in MBA business plan competitions around the country. In the spring of 2010, Keith's team and business plan won first place in the International New Ventures Competition at the University of Nebraska and received a check for seven thousand dollars in prize money.

Not missing a beat, the team decided to use their winnings to bankroll High Road Craft Ice Cream & Sorbet and buy a modest pilot ice cream machine to start sampling their product. From there, Keith convinced a number of his MBA colleagues to invest in the new venture. By the time he had finished talking to people; Keith had raised over two hundred and fifty thousand dollars in start-up capital.

He had never intended his little company to market to retail organizations. His plan was to simply fill the void in the restaurant ice cream market. However, a fateful phone call placed by one of his business partners changed everything for High Road. One day his partner, Hunter, decided to call up Whole Foods, a high-end grocery chain, to see what the process would be to put their ice cream in Whole Foods stores. As a result, Keith and Hunter wound up with an extraordinary opportunity.

Keith was making samples one day when Hunter mentioned that there were going to be some people from Whole Foods stopping by to taste their product. Keith didn't think much of it. He knew that Hunter had called them previously to find out the process involved in trying to get the ice cream on the company's shelves. Keith assumed that the people who came were some sort of lower-level bureaucrats. He had no idea that the casually dressed group who raved about his ice cream included the vice president of Procurement and all other important decision-makers in the Whole Foods organization.

> *Lesson Learned: All it took was a belief in his abilities and one phone call, and Keith Schroeder built a business around gourmet ice cream.*

The rest, as they say, is history. From that one phone call, High Road Craft Ice Cream & Sorbet is now on the shelves of an entire region of Whole Food stores. All it took was a belief in his abilities and one phone call, and Keith Schroeder built a business around gourmet ice cream.

CHAPTER 14
Tim Eippert
CEO and Owner MC Sign

"The bankruptcy papers were on his desk."

"I'm afraid of the sight of blood!"

—TIM EIPPERT

Tim Eippert comes from a family of doctors. His father and two brothers are physicians, so it's amazing that he didn't become one too. When asked why he didn't follow his family's career path, he told the truth. "I'm afraid of the sight of blood!" Entrepreneurship was his calling.

Tim always had the entrepreneurial bug. He started a lawn mowing business when he was sixteen, and it wasn't just the next door neighbor's yards he worked on; he had business all over town. That's when he learned how to manage money, schedule jobs, and actually be responsible as a sixteen-year-old boy.

Tim went on to graduate from Kent State University with a degree in business, and he caught the entrepreneurial spirit from his professors. While he was a college sophomore, Tim got a job at a sign repair company. He would ride around at night, taking pictures of companies that needed sign repair. The next day, he would ask for their business. Often, Tim was successful. One day, he visited Sun Appliances and actually acquired the repair business. It happened to be the biggest order his employer ever received.

In 1994, while in his early twenties, he bought MC Sign in Ashtabula, Ohio. Its revenues were about one hundred thousand dollars a year, but Tim was thinking big. In his eyes, that was an incredibly small company. His plans were for a multi-million-dollar organization that would sell and repair signs nationally. There was only one small problem: Tim had no money. So with about a thousand dollars and a Discover Card, this hopeful entrepreneur was going to change the world.

Tim was twenty-four and wet behind the ears, and he needed a business edge. He did something that, over the long term, was a key to success. He developed an advisory board for the company, and with the help of a college professor board member, Tim asked a few big corporate names to advise him. The board helped him with a selling strategy and introduced Tim to some potentially big customers.

The first three years in business, his company grew rapidly, but that wasn't necessarily a good thing. Managing the cash flow became a serious company issue. Lots of things went wrong, and suddenly things took such a turn for the worse that the bankruptcy papers were on his desk, ready to be signed.

He'd risked big, and he was about to pay the price of failure. Then, like a gift from heaven, he got a large sign order from U. S. Bank, and the rest, as they say, is history. The papers were not signed. They were shredded, and the company became profitable, with good cash flow. For the next three years, business doubled every year. Now Tim's vision came true. MC Sign became a national company.

At this writing, Tim's company has revenues north of fifty million dollars a year, with well over a hundred employees. Now that's success! The daily sacrifices of the early years paid off, and there are a lot of people that are quite happy he didn't quit. Especially his hundred employees!

Tim's secret of success? There isn't just one. But his persistence in moving the business forward and obtaining large customers is part of it. One thing is for sure. There were times Tim wanted to quit, but he never gave up. He always had that vision of being a national company with very good revenues, and he made that dream came true.

Entrepreneurs like Tim are a very interesting bunch. The successful ones are not afraid to fail, and if they do, they forget about their failures and continue to keep on keeping on. They are in a constant learning mode, reading business books and talking to their mentors and advisors frequently.

Tim's creating his advisory board was one of the best things he ever did, but his learning didn't stop there. He knew he had to continue to "sharpen the saw," so Tim joined The Executive Committee, later named Vistage. It's a group of CEOs who meet once per month to talk about business issues.

He sharpened his skills by talking to other business people, and he learned many of his management ideas from his associations. One of the reasons for MC Sign's success, and one that Tim developed from the beginning, was to build a company culture that is customer-driven. If you ask Tim today why his company is so successful, his quick reply is, "Great service."

There are dozens of competitor sign companies, but MC Sign's service is the best. Tim has thirty or more customer service centers around the country, partnering with subcontractors. He quotes a service time of three days but almost always completes the service requests more quickly. In a given quarter, Tim's average repair time is two and a half days. I think that's called under-promising and over-delivering! No wonder the company is so successful.

The Great Recession of 2008 to 2011 crushed many sign companies. Most of the industry was 20 percent down in revenues. Not MC Sign! It *grew* at 20 percent every year. Tim's laser focus on the customer was instrumental in the company's growth during that time, but there are other reasons as well.

During the recession, his management team decided not to cut the marketing budget, and MC Sign still attended all the needed industry conventions while some of its competitors stayed at home. Again, Tim took the risk in uncertain times, and his gamble paid off in spades.

When asked what advice he would give someone who wanted to start a business, Tim said, "Find something you are good at and stick to it." Tim found something and stuck to it, and it's wildly successful.

There are two tipping points that got Tim to where he is today. First, he wouldn't have gone into the sign business if it weren't for selling repairs to Sun Appliance. Second, his business boomed because of U. S. Bank's big order. These are two tipping points that Tim will always remember. Without their having happened, he might not be in business today.

Tim Eippert: Persistent. Patient. Driven to succeed.

CHAPTER 15
Sharon Ward
Co-Founder of Northcoast
Senior Moving

*Risking That Retirement
Account for a Dream*

"We're not leaving here until your toothbrush is where you are used to seeing it and your slippers are under your bed and your TV is working."

—**SHARON WARD**

Was Sharon Ward a crazy person who did a seemingly radical thing? After twenty-seven plus years in corporate America, working as a banker, Sharon and her husband Ron decided to start a company that specialized in moving senior citizens.

The vision of Northcoast Senior Moving evolved when both of Ron's parents became ill and were unable to care for themselves. The family was faced with putting two loved ones into assisted living. Sharon and Ron found that the process of moving not one but both parents out of the family home, while they raised children and conducted their own family business, became an extraordinary undertaking.

There were dozens of tasks and jobs that needed to be coordinated. In order to get things done, they were making time-consuming phone calls for this, that, and the other, all over the place. Every piece of the process was made much more difficult because there was no real point person to call to get things coordinated. This responsibility was overwhelming.

After doing this extraordinary amount of work to get their parents moved, Sharon and Ron realized that they couldn't be the only people on earth facing this issue. They sat down and started talking. What about those who don't even live near their parents anymore? What about the ins and outs of liquidating real estate? How would you even begin to spearhead the process of a life-changing move from five states away?

Sharon and Ron were blazing new trails. There was certainly no business model for what they were trying to accomplish. They wanted to avoid being something akin to Allied Van Lines for seniors. They went step-by-step through the process that they had undergone with their own parents. They did research into what resources they would have to develop. Sharon and Ron were not simply picking up grandma

"Because of my conservative nature, I was very concerned about making sure that this worked. But when you believe in something and have a passion, it is made a little bit easier, because I knew that I was putting it in the right place."

and moving her from point A to point B. Ryder trucks could do that. What they were talking about was a process that was much more involved and that constituted a lot more hand-holding.

Through their discussions and research, they devised a system that would ensure they were effectively servicing and overseeing the complete process. It covered issues starting with selling the home but also involved finding a new suitable and affordable place for the client to move to. They learned how to consult with clients on problems such as this: "I am moving from a two thousand-square-foot home to a five hundred-square-foot room in an assisted living facility. What do I take with me? What about all of my precious possessions that I can't fit into my new home? What do I do with them?"

Sharon and Ron put a lot of time and effort into coming up with their system, and the moment of truth was getting near. They needed some capital to get their baby off the ground. Remember, Sharon was a banker. Bankers make their living off of leveraging risk. But she did something very unbanker like. They agreed that they were not going to go into debt to get the company off the ground. It was either going to work through their sweat and inspiration, or they would both go back to the banking world.

Sharon and Ron took twenty thousand dollars from a retirement account and hit the market. They had reservations, but when it came down to moving ahead with the business, both believed deeply in what they were doing. Today, Northcoast Senior Moving is profitable and growing rapidly. Sharon and Ron are now able to take their earnings and reinvest them back into the company.

Sharon's lesson learned is this: If you really believe in yourself and have a passion for your idea, good things can happen. ***Yes, even a banker, who has to deal with all kinds of rules and regulations, can become an entrepreneur.***

CHAPTER 16
Ryan Carroll
President Lake City Plating

Into the Fire!

"I believe in working hard when you sometimes don't need to in order to prevent problems before they start."

—RYAN CARROLL

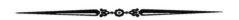

College is a time of new beginnings and excitement in many young people's lives. Most college bound kids get to leave home and live in a bubble. There are parties, nights out with friends, activities, and finally, studies. For many, the college experience is a neat utopia from which they have to be dragged kicking and screaming...to the real world. This is Ryan Carroll's story. Snatched from his little Shangri-La and thrust into adulthood in a seemingly cruel manner, Ryan had to learn to run with the big boys...quickly.

It is 2001. Ryan is in the middle of his sophomore year at Kent State University in Kent, Ohio. The phone rings. It's his mom. She needs help running Lake City Plating, the family business she had taken over nine years ago when Ryan's dad passed away. Lake City Plating is a company that specializes in putting protective coatings on metal parts. At this point, the company is nowhere near profitable, and she wants to turn it around. She asks Ryan to come home and help make it happen.

Ryan returned. He was somewhat familiar with Lake City Plating from working there at a summer job when he was in high school, but as a twenty-year-old college dropout, he was unprepared to jump into the fire. Ryan had to deal with a cold, hard reality: either help fix the financial issues or the business would be jeopardized.

Ryan faced an enormous challenge. He sat down and tried to figure out what had been going wrong with the company. He looked at all of the customers and the pricing on orders. Ryan discovered that there were some customers who had been getting sweetheart deals, and Lake City Plating was losing a ton of money on each one.

Ryan did what he had to do, knowing what the probable outcome would be. He upped the pricing for the next set of orders, in some instances, as much as three hundred percent. He had to. The company couldn't continue to give the product away. As he feared, sales from those customers plummeted. Before long, about two-thirds of them left for competitors.

Fast-forward nine months. Ryan had been there for the better part of a year and didn't take a paycheck. This was a simple and easy decision. Even with Ryan's limited business experience, he knew that he couldn't pay himself if the company didn't have the resources. So Ryan had kept working for free, seventy hours a week. He was exhausted.

Since Ryan didn't know the "ins and outs" of business, he needed to spend more time on the job learning. As hard as it was in the beginning, Ryan admits that he loved what he was doing. His efforts were making a difference.

> *"Work on issues that will make your company profitable, not things that do not contribute to the bottom line."*

With his back against the wall, Ryan picked up a copy of the Thomas Register, a gigantic listing of manufacturers in the United

States, and started making phone calls. That's right—Ryan started cold-calling over the phone. What he found was a whole new world of business. One by one, new clients were added.

Ryan discovered that by purging Lake City Plating of its unprofitable clients and bringing on new customers who were more suited to Lake City's strengths, he had created a more solid foundation on which the company could grow. And grow it did.

Ten years later, Lake City Plating was booming. The great recession, which devastated much of the manufacturing industry in the United States, proved to be an unworthy opponent for the Carroll family business. Ryan found ways to deftly navigate through the worst of times in the manufacturing sector. He has since had much of the company automated.

Lake City Plating bears little resemblance to the company Ryan took over. Today, the company has been named one of the Cleveland area's top one hundred fastest growing businesses by Case Western Reserve University's Weatherhead School of Management.

The eighty-hour workweeks are gone. Ryan jokes that now he only has to work fifty-hour weeks because, finally, he knows what he is doing. Thrust into a seemingly no-win situation, green and naïve, Ryan demonstrated that through analysis, innovation, and hard work he could not only survived but thrive!

Secret to Success: Don't be afraid to fire customers who aren't worth the effort or who are unprofitable. For Ryan Carroll, it took courage, but it started Lake City Plating's path to profitability.

CHAPTER 17
Tim Dimoff
Founder and CEO of
SACS Consulting

The Beatings Had to Stop

Bottom line is, my body just couldn't take the beatings anymore..."

—TIM DIMOFF

Entrepreneurs are a diverse group. They decide to take the plunge into being their own bosses for a bevy of reasons: they get fired from their job, they retire and start their own businesses, or they find a unique niche or market that they feel is completely untapped. The stream of reasons to go out on your own is seemingly endless. But what would you say if I told you that the reason that Tim Dimoff started SACS was because if he had stayed in his regular job, he would either wind up in a wheelchair or dead?

Tim spent eighteen years in the Akron, Ohio, police department. He was a beat cop, served on the SWAT team, was an undercover policeman, and finally served as a narcotics officer. Let's just say that he chose a rather dangerous profession. Tim has the scars to prove it. In his eighteen years of taking vermin off of the streets, he had seven major injuries. His final fight put him in rehab for a year with a broken back and jaw. You see, if Tim didn't switch professions, he wasn't going to be around very long.

During his rehab, Tim realized a stark contrast. He went from having some extraordinarily busy days catching criminals to being bored...very bored. Rehab gives you some time to think. Tim decided that he was done with law enforcement, at least in his current capacity. He couldn't keep doing this. His body just wouldn't stand up to the physical challenge. It was time for a change. In his daily trips back and forth from the rehab facility to his home, he would think to himself, "What do I know? What is my knowledge base? Where can I go from here? I know a lot about narcotics and drugs. I know a lot about litigation and testifying." Tim also knew a lot about education and training because he had been training his fellow officers for years. He thought to himself about how he could accentuate what he was really good at, what he had experience with, and apply it to the business world.

Unable to come to any real conclusions about his experiences and where they could take him in the private sector, Tim did know one thing. The name of the game in any profession is relationships and relationship management. He decided to join the local chamber of commerce. The chamber gave him a list of around one hundred business people in the community considered to be sharp, established, and up and coming. It was from this list that Tim planned to do some market research.

"I'd really like to meet you for a breakfast, lunch, or cup of coffee and just pick your brain for a little bit—even if it is at your office for fifteen minutes and ask you some questions. I'm looking for some direction and guidance, and you've been identified as someone who can help me."

He did something totally unique. He would call up a contact person from the list and tell them that he or she had been identified as one of the stronger business leaders and business minds in the community. He would say that this person's company had been identified as a company on the rise and that he'd like to meet the person for a breakfast, lunch, or cup of coffee and just pick his or her brain for a little bit, even if it was just for fifteen minutes at the person's office. He was "looking for some direction and guidance," and this person had been identified as one of the best that could help him. Ninety percent of the calls he made resulted in a sit-down meeting with the businessperson.

Tim began to get a general idea of what he wanted to do. Through all of his research, he discovered multiple ways in which someone with his knowledge and expertise could help some of these businesses. His services would include, but not be limited to, workplace violence, bullying, drug and alcohol issues, security, human resource issues, people not getting along, and the building of positive cultures. In all of the conversations he had, he was able to bounce ideas off these business people and shape what could be done as a service. He even got a handful of customers immediately as well as referrals for future business. From then on, SACS Consulting was born.

Then his company grew. Tim branched the company off in all sorts of directions. When asked what his "secret sauce" is for being so successful, he will tell you that it is the building of solid relationships. Once his company gets its foot in the door, it establishes customers for life. SACS Consulting boasts a 93 percent customer retention rate. Clients don't leave him because he provides a good service, and he makes sure that SACS Consulting is at the top of his clients' minds.

> *Lesson learned: Relationships **do** matter. In a consulting business, the relationships with clients are vital for the long-term success of the business.*

Tim utilizes a system of touches to make sure that his company is not forgotten in the everyday lives of those who utilize his services. He does this through newsletters and other outreach methods utilizing social media. To Tim, there is a fine line between keeping your company on the top of your prospective clients' minds and "polluting" them. SACS Consulting is very careful in this regard. Tim preaches the importance of personal relationships in keeping his business. Newsletters and social media are excellent tools. They can be very effective in maintaining and growing business. But for effective businesses, they cannot and will not ever be a replacement for personal relationships. Tim believes that these relationships are still the backbone of business.

"If I haven't met you and I don't know you and I don't have any personal connection to you, it is very easy for me to leave you as a client."

—Tim Dimoff

Being the serial entrepreneur that he is, Tim has branched his services off in several different directions. As each embodies what he has envisioned and becomes profitable, he sells it off. It is safe to say that Tim has done pretty well for himself. Currently he gives speeches nationally; has authored six books on security; has been seen regularly on CNN, Dateline NBC, and FOX; and has been heard on a variety of radio programs.

From a narcotics detective to entrepreneur. An incredible success story of self-analysis and finding a niche.

CHAPTER 18
Roger Sustar
Founder of Fredon Corporation

"Forty-six years and still learning"

"If you want to start a company and only look to get rich, you'll go broke."

—ROGER SUSTAR

Fredon Corporation was a tiny Ohio manufacturer until it was purchased by Roger Sustar. Roger and a partner each borrowed seven thousand dollars from a bank to buy the company, and Roger didn't know if he would survive the first year. The business flourished; however, Roger doesn't want to take any credit for its success. But employees and manufacturing friends believe that Roger *is* and always *will* be the driving force that makes Fredon a winner.

Years ago, after he got out of the army, Roger went to work for his father, and that lasted a total of two days. He wasn't fired; Roger quit. He had the manufacturing bug, and he wanted to prove to his father that he could be as successful in his own business. He bought Fredon Corporation.

Fredon went through many ups and downs, like all manufacturers do. Roger endured recessions and customers outsourcing to China and to other countries in the Far East. Like many small-business owners, Roger found that his bank at one time wanted to foreclose on a large loan. Roger fought back. The banker saw that Roger had the tenacity to survive and stopped the foreclosure proceedings.

Business challenges completely out of his control arose consistently. Fredon became certified to build parts for the aerospace industry. After September 11, 2001, all aerospace orders vanished. In fact, Fredon was even getting some orders returned. One was over one hundred thousand dollars in value. During that time, everyone in the organization took substantial pay cuts. Then Roger's team got together to make new strategic decisions, and his business returned.

Through thick and thin, Roger succeeded by hiring good people who had a strong work ethic. Roger learned from his experiences and used as much data as he could find and then let his intuition take over. That's one of his secrets to success.

Here's another secret to this entrepreneur's success. When faced with business issues, especially strategic ones, he counsels new entrepreneurs **not** to go with their emotions. He insists that "Entrepreneurs shouldn't let their hearts get in the way of making good decisions. That only works in love. Go with statistics. The numbers don't lie."

"Entrepreneurs shouldn't let their hearts get in the way of making good decisions. That only works in love. Go with statistics. The numbers don't lie."

You can visit Roger at his plant at 6:00 a.m. and 6:00 p.m. Even after forty years in business, he usually works a sixty-hour week, which probably is another secret to his success. Through this hard work, Roger has created one of the best manufacturing firms in the Midwest.

In today's manufacturing world, one of the biggest challenges is finding qualified people to hire. At this writing, there are thousands of employees at manufacturing plants around the country who are or will be retiring in the years ahead. Finding their replacements is now a pressing problem.

What is there to do about this very persistent and serious issue? Enter Roger Sustar, the entrepreneur and problem solver. Roger began an organization called **The Alliance for Working Together (AWT)**, which recruited paid members who are owners of other manufacturing firms, and he worked with them to develop technical courses at a local community college.

He also solicited donations from the community to provide scholarships for young men and women who normally couldn't afford to go to school. It's working. The AWT organization now provides tours of local manufacturing companies to thousands of high school students. The group explains the industry profile and image to people who would never have known about the possibilities of earning an exceptionally good income in an excellent manufacturing environment.

Through Roger's donors, his dues-paying members, and good community college courses as well as his drive to make this program successful, the AWT program could be a new paradigm in technical education for young high school graduates throughout the United States. His initiatives are sowing the seeds for future manufacturing employees.

"If the government will just stay out of our way, we will take this country to greater heights."

By the way, Roger takes no salary for his work at AWT. As he says, he "isn't the only small-business owner who gives his or her heart and mind to other entrepreneurs."

For all the work that Roger does in the community and for his industry, he has never stopped learning. Even after four decades in the business, his reading list is extensive. Roger's work with congressmen and senators still fuels his fire. He firmly believes that the private sector's vitality is very important to our country and to our allies in the free world. His mantra is, "Please get government out of our way, and we will take this country to greater heights."

Today, many people who want to start a small business ask Roger for his advice. He always says, "If you are looking to just get rich, you'll go broke. If you want to do something different, invent something new, and try to solve a problem, you'll be successful."

Roger Sustar: Survivor. Visionary. Hard Worker.

CHAPTER 19
Mario Jurcic
Founder of Secure IT Asset
Disposition Services

---

*Sandals with Shorts and a
T-shirt with Pizza Stains*

"I didn't have a strategy. My idea was that I needed to get a two thousand-square-foot facility and figure out what I was doing."

—MARIO JURCIC.

Sometimes it seems we are following a path that has already been planned for us. Such is the story of one Mario Jurcic and Secure IT Asset Disposition Services. Mario was destined to become an entrepreneur.

Mario's parents immigrated to the United States from Croatia. His upbringing was not unlike that of a lot of second-generation immigrants to this country. His parents were hard workers who spent every waking hour in the family machine shop. On Saturdays, Mario and his mom would go to the shop and clean all day. Between schoolwork and the machine shop responsibilities, he took little time to socialize. A strong work ethic was ingrained in his DNA.

After graduating from high school and before heading off to college, Mario found a warehouse job where he worked in the surplus machinery division for a local scrapyard. It wasn't glamorous work, but he loved it. The dirty industrial environment was what he had grown accustomed to since playing around in his father's shop as a kid. The scrapyard paychecks would help him begin to pay for college expenses.

Mario arrived one morning to find that the scrapyard was the proud new custodian of a whole bunch of outdated, used computers.

Employees had a lot of experience disposing of all sorts of different machinery parts, but no one in the warehouse had ever dealt with getting rid of computers. No one had any idea of what to do with them, since the hard drives still contained sensitive information.

Mario was the only person in the shop who understood the serious legalities of the situation. He knew that the data could not be left in the format it was in. Some of that information was retrievable simply by booting up the computer. If any of the personal data got into the wrong hands, there could have been huge problems, including some very large lawsuits. This was when Mario found out what it was to love what you do. He fell in love with the recycling business.

Amazingly enough, not one of the company executives realized that this dilemma presented a need. Mario did. He researched the issue and devised a way to dispose of the computers without compromising the information within them. What an accomplishment for an eighteen-year-old who hadn't started college!

Secure IT Asset Disposition Services was born. It was originally called E-scrap. Mario started his business with seven hundred dollars, which was all the money he had in the world (pretty good for a college kid). It would have to do. Mario wasn't interested in courting financiers or venture capitalists or going from bank to bank looking for small-business loans. He wanted to truly do it himself.

Then fortune happened. Mario was in a computer lab helping a friend with his résumé when he saw a bunch of old computers being removed. When he asked where they were going, he was told to talk with the purchasing agent for the department. Mario decided to strike up a conversation with him. Dressed in sandals, shorts, and a T-shirt with pizza stains all over it, Mario knew exactly what he wanted to do: dispose of the college computers to prevent personal information from being accessed. He earmarked this purchasing agent to help him jump-start his new company.

At first the purchasing agent was leery of Mario, but soon he took a liking to this young, aggressive student. Mario was brutally honest and simply explained how there was no chance he would be able to start his new business without this person's help. He posed the ultimate question: "What do I have to do to get the business?" A bold question for a young college student to ask.

> *"What do I have to do to get the business? A bold question for a young college student to ask."*

Now the rest is history. The purchasing agent gave Mario the business of disposing of the college's old computers, and Mario has since turned his company into a multi-million-dollar organization. He has even been celebrated at the White House for being one of the elite, under thirty Empact 100 entrepreneurs in the United States.

Mario has a bundle of energy, and because of that family DNA, he knows how to work hard. But his real secret to success is that he's in the customers' faces all the time. He's up-front with them, and it's appreciated. His being close to his customers has built relationships that will last a long time, both personally and professionally.

Mario Jurcic: Hard worker. Customer Focused. Driven.

CHAPTER 20
Keith Kokal

Founder of Micro Laboratories, Inc.

Always Looking. Always Working. Always Learning.

"They could rob me of my belongings but not my knowledge."

—KEITH KOKAL

Keith grew up in the worst part of town and never graduated from high school. He was shot and stabbed, and he learned how to fight, to take a punch, and survive. Every day, danger and violent crime was prevalent in his neighborhood. Not a great way to start out life.

Many nights, Keith went to bed hungry. At the age of eight, to earn money for food, Keith started his own shoeshine business. He used an old wooden pallet to make his shoeshine box for storing his shining brushes, waxes, and pastes. Then Keith went to tough neighborhood bars at night and shone shoes for anyone willing to pay him a quarter. The shoeshine business was Keith's first entrepreneurial experience but certainly not his last. He learned to deal with people, negotiate, watch every penny, **and be able to eat**.

His next venture was an electronics business. Keith bought an old radio and TV tube tester from a pawn shop and set up business in a small room at the back of his parents' home. The neighbors would send their televisions and radios to be fixed. Keith tested the old tubes and replaced them, and voila—they worked! That was his first project in the high-tech world. Even more important, he continued to learn about business and people.

All of Keith Kokal's childhood struggles helped him become an entrepreneur. Hardship, poverty, and the will to survive helped him find the confidence to succeed in business. Even after being shot, stabbed, and robbed at gunpoint, nothing was going to stop Keith from being successful. He says, "They could take away my belongings, but they couldn't steal my knowledge. I was going to learn everything I could to get away from poverty and get the hell out of here." And that's what he did.

After dropping out of high school at fifteen, Keith went to work for an auto parts store, where he learned all he could about cars and the auto parts business. He ended up repairing and selling cars **before** he got his driver's license. He would sell them for cash and put the money in his socks, just in case someone tried to rob him on his long walk home.

Then, after ten years of changing jobs, each with better pay, he started Micro Laboratories, calibrating inspection equipment. He developed the idea of a calibration company from being a quality manager at an aerospace company. Keith wasn't satisfied with the contractors who were calibrating delicate equipment. He decided that the industry needed to change. Keith worked for the aerospace company during the day and served his clients at night and on weekends.

Keith struggled to get his business off the ground. He laughs about his first big order. He got up at 4:30 in the morning, drove fifty miles one way, calibrated some very sensitive gauges, and then drove back to his day job. **Then the customer didn't pay!** Keith jokingly says that instead of the invoice reading as "net thirty," the bill should have read "net never!"

His company needed seed money, so Keith sold his rental home. The fifteen thousand-dollar profit was used to purchase testing equipment, and his business grew. Today, Micro Laboratories, with over two thousand clients, is established in the field of gauge calibration and performs work for both small businesses and Fortune 500 companies. Not bad for a kid from the streets.

How did Keith Kokal become so successful? Yes, he worked hard and was inspired to succeed by his challenging childhood, but there is something else Keith does to be successful. He keeps learning by reading good business books.

Rich Dad, Poor Dad, by Robert Kiyosaki, is at the top of his list of excellent entrepreneurship books. He suggests that this book should be taught in all high schools. It would give our students an actual lesson in free enterprise and would help them understand the real world of financial management.

"Instead of typing out the invoice as net thirty, the bill should have said 'net never.'"

Because of his talents, Keith is now one of the foremost metrologists (practitioners of the science of measurement) in the Midwest. He is a senior member of the American Society for Quality and a charter member of the Measurement Quality Division. Today, Micro Laboratories is recognized throughout the world.

Keith's success proves that you can be poor and disadvantaged and not be a college graduate and still become a very successful entrepreneur.

Keith Kokal: Always working. Always looking. Always learning.

CHAPTER 21
Andy McCartney
Owner of Bowden Manufacturing

Community Service and Great Teammates

"We realized that when you ask what you are looking for in a teammate, the last thing on people's minds is that they be a great CNC machinist."

—ANDY MCCARTNEY

Andy McCartney has owned Bowden Manufacturing for ten years. He is an impressive guy with a notable background. Andy is a graduate of the United States Naval Academy. He spent the better part of several years as an officer on the aircraft carrier USS *Enterprise*.

It is important to talk about Andy McCartney, not for these reasons but for how he keeps a productive, happy, winning culture at Bowden Manufacturing and most important, how he continues to give to his community.

Andy's father bought an interest in Bowden in the early 1970s, and Andy bought him out several years ago. He is big on a positive workplace culture. Much of how this former naval officer operates his company is reflective of his military background.

Skills are nice. They help you to be successful in what you do; however, they are not as important as your willingness and ability to be a team player. You can have all the skills in the world, but if you are not interested in doing what needs to be done for the sake of the end results, then you are not going to last very long at Bowden. The interviewing process at Andy's company is thorough, but he leaves the final decision on new hires to his employees.

They all vote on who they think would fit best in the position to be filled.

Several years ago, one of Bowden's main clients informed Andy that it was going to place a series of big orders. Andy knew that the company was at a point where he would have to start hiring more people to deal with the increase in business. Andy went to his employees and asked them to try to figure out the best evaluation process. He asked the million-dollar question: "What are you looking for in a teammate?"

Andy split his coworkers into seven teams to brainstorm. His employees ended up spending six weeks defining what they believed a teammate should be and what they should look for in the hiring process. The results were fascinating.

"We have our teammates around whoever is being reviewed to get kind of a grade. We grade each other on our teammate qualities — myself included."

Previously, if you were to ask Andy what to look for in hiring a new CNC machinist, he would have said that he or she had to be a **great** CNC machinist. After team discussions, the qualities the coworkers desired included other priorities: Were the prospective hires trustworthy? Were they safety conscious? Were they team players? Were they good communicators? Did they have a positive attitude and a strong work ethic? Were they responsible? Were they dependable? Were they patient? Were they disciplined? Were they willing to learn? The fact that a candidate was a great machinist fell from the most important quality to last on the list.

These values are so important to the team at Bowden that each week one is picked for discussion at team meetings. Andy wants to make sure that he is reinforcing what is important with his staff. He also has gone so far as to make sure that all of these values are part of each employee's performance review. When teammates are up for a yearly review, they not only are graded by Andy but by all others in the unit. If there is a discrepancy between what Andy and his coworkers think, the team gets together to figure out why they're on different pages.

Guess who else is subject to this team performance review? Andy himself! The very fact that Andy scrapped the top-down approach to hiring and evaluating employees really allowed those who work at Bowden to feel as if they were part of a team. Everyone is given a sense of ownership in the organization. All feel as if they have a vested interest in doing well and getting the job done.

In 2011, Bowden Manufacturing was named the Chamber of Commerce Business of the Year for Willoughby, Ohio. This was not for doing a good job providing products for local area businesses but for the extensive community service **Bowden** performs by supporting local charities. This is Andy's top priority. He is on the board of directors of the Cleveland chapter of the Ronald McDonald House, where he and his employees go to the facility once a quarter to serve meals.

When asked about the company's involvement in the community, Andy tells a story about when Bowden first got involved with Ronald McDonald House. At the facility, one of his team leaders

> *"They all went out on the field, and he threw out the first pitch. He was absolutely off the chart excited and happy."*

was introduced to a completely bald nine-year-old boy who was running around the room. To look at that young man's energy level, you would never have thought he was going through cancer treatment. The kid was also a huge baseball fan.

Andy decided to get him some tickets to a game played by the local Lake County Captains, the minor league team affiliate of the Cleveland Indians. Andy made a couple of phone calls, and within days, the boy was throwing out the first pitch at a game. He had the time of his life. Giving back not only feels good for Andy and Bowden Manufacturing but for his work teams as well.

Bowden is just one example of how small business is not only the backbone of the economy but is in many ways the backbone of charitable giving and volunteering in America. Andy puts things in simple perspective: "Once you see kids going through these unbelievable circumstances, it gives us perspective and helps us put our efforts to good use."

Andy McCartney: Innovator. Giver. Teammate.

CHAPTER 22
Tony Bass
CEO of Super Lawn Technologies

The System Is the Solution

"I looked at myself in the mirror and said, 'Wow, you own a broken company. So what are you going to do about it? Are you going to go to work fixing it or change your job, or will you simply live with the status quo?'"

—TONY BASS

A landscaping business, like many others, can be very challenging. Scores of people try their hands in this field, only to find that their bottom lines don't allow them to thrive for a very long time. Many of the companies that do survive seem just to be hanging on by their fingernails. Swallowed up by the industry, Tony Bass was in the latter group.

Working long days jockeying a shovel and lengthy nights marketing the company, Tony became excited when a nice chunk of money was collected. His disappointment was considerable when he realized that most of that money (or in some instances, more) would have to go right back out the door. That was the arduous roller coaster he rode for the first five years of Bass Custom Landscapes' existence.

Tony's business began in central Georgia, not the most densely populated stretch of real estate on the planet. His home county had barely one hundred thousand people, and the surrounding counties were not much more populous. Simply put, it was a small market.

Tony wasn't exactly prepared to jump in with both feet either. His financial situation certainly didn't appear to be one that should, could, or would fund a burgeoning multi-million-dollar company. Tony jokes about it now, but when he started, he literally had four hundred dollars that wasn't even in cash. It was in stock of Winn Dixie (a supermarket chain in the southeast).

Tony was educated, but not in the way that he really needed to be. He had taken a number of courses in college that helped him with portions of what he would be dealing with on a day in and day out basis. Unfortunately, he had zero experience in both the business world and in the landscaping industry.

A few years went by, and Bass Custom Landscapes brought in a decent client base. The company was bringing in between three and four hundred thousand dollars per year in revenue and providing good service to its clients. The problem was that the cash flow was barely OK,

"It seemed that every time that money would come in, there would be a reason or cause for it to go right back out."

and profitability was very shaky. Tony hadn't devised a way to keep some of that money that was coming in from going right back out the door in the form of other expenses.

Tony admitted there were a lot of company protocols and processes that just didn't seem efficient or helpful to the bottom line. One day after reading Michael E. Gerber's *The E-Myth Revisited*, a book about the importance of company organization, Tony had an epiphany.

He came up with a structure to fix his broken business. To do this, Tony did something extreme—he went on a sabbatical. He stopped accepting new clients. During the day, when the phone rang, Tony wouldn't pick up calls. At night, he returned those that had to do with the future of his company. Tony retained only the core group of clients that Bass had been servicing through lawn maintenance contracts (mowing, trimming, and pruning). He did this for six months.

The time off proved to be priceless. Tony became a real student not only of his own company but of the lawn-care industry as a whole. When he took a step back and observed what was happening around him, everything became clearer. As he looked at how everything was done in

> *"I think that most people just get super busy, and they never focus on working on the business. They focus on working in the business."*

his company, from the way the work was completed to how new employees should be trained, innovative ideas surfaced.

Tony devised a way to fix the problem of storing, organizing, and then protecting the equipment from theft once it left the shop. Next, Tony took a stopwatch and calculated how long it took to complete the equipment loading onto the trucks and trailers. He also looked at the hookup time for the variety of trailers that were attached to pickup trucks.

Finally, Tony went through and reassessed what every employee's role should be in the company, from the office staff to the landscape maintenance technicians, the landscape construction technicians, the designers, and the mechanics who repaired and maintained the equipment. After six months of reviewing every position, Tony created a document that was more than four hundred pages in length. It was the road map to **Bass Custom Landscape's** success.

Until Tony Bass struck, the only way to get equipment to the job site was via the use of a pickup truck and trailer. Tony hated having to utilize trailers. When the crews got to the job sites, the trailers had to be backed into driveways. So invariably, Tony would have to spend time training personnel to perform these maneuvers without backing over curbs, lampposts, mailboxes, etc. Also, the trailers were generally wide open, so if someone was not watching, the equipment placed on them (such as blowers, lawn mowers, and trimmers) could very easily be stolen.

Then one day the ultimate embarrassment happened. A crew was driving on a four-lane highway. The truck's driver had failed to secure the trailer properly, so the entire trailer mechanism disengaged from the hitch, and the trailer went flying. It crossed over the median through two more lanes of oncoming traffic and smashed through the exterior fencing of a local air force base. By some miracle, it struck no cars, and no one was injured.

This was a true wake-up call for Tony. He needed to figure out how he could eliminate trailers from the day-to-day operations of his growing lawn business. Tony felt a personal responsibility to both the public and his employees to make a safer transport vehicle. He decided to design his own work truck, one that would not utilize a trailer.

The Super Lawn Truck was born. Tony devised a way to convert an enclosed commercial grade work truck into a rolling warehouse trailer/billboard/security system. The truck also sported a tool organization system that kept all gear secure for transport. Finally, it was entirely enclosed, ensuring that neither the elements nor unscrupulous passersby could separate the equipment from the truck.

Michael E. Gerber's *The E-Myth Revisited* changed Tony's company and his life. Through Gerber's advice, Tony adjusted to the market, and through hard work, another company, Super Lawn Trucks, was born. Tony now manufactures and sells these fifty thousand-dollar trucks in forty-two states across America and in Canada—all because Tony took his sabbatical from his lawn-care business. Michael E. Gerber should be very proud! Tony Bass' secret to success was having the courage to rethink his business and find a system that worked. This led to a new product that revolutionized the industry.

CHAPTER 23
Arline Kneen
Founder of Traveline

*Forty-Nine Dollars
and a Hunch!*

World's Oldest Travel Agent
I've probably been there...

– ARLINE KNEEN

The above words are on Arline Kneen's business card. She is ninety-six years old. Honest! If it is on planet earth, then she probably has been there, from North Africa to the Far East to the frozen desolation of Antarctica. For

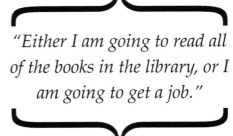

"Either I am going to read all of the books in the library, or I am going to get a job."

all seven continents and everywhere in between, Arline has the knowledge and expertise to talk about anywhere in the world.

Arleen is the ultimate travel consultant. Not only can she tell you what to do, where to eat, and what to see, but Arline makes sure that her clients know what to experience and what to avoid. This no-nonsense, frank, and honest approach has kept the northeastern Ohio travelers returning to her for the past fifty years.

In 1962 Arline had an itch. She was in her early forties, and like so many women in the United States during the fifties and sixties, Arline was a homemaker whose primary role had been that of a wife and mother. She was aware of the gender roles that her generation had established, but that didn't mean that she liked them...or intended to play by those rules.

One day her husband Bob walked through the door and saw a giant pile of library books sitting on the floor. Bob asked, "What's this all about?" Arline replied, "I'm either going to read all the books in the library, or I'm going to get a job." Bob expressed his concern about Arline embarking on a real-world career. After all, she hadn't had a job since before they'd had children. This made the red hair on the back of Arline's neck stand up in frustration. Bob continued, "What could you do? You've been out of the job market for so long." Arline responded, "***Watch me!***"

Arline's first business endeavor was a restaurant called The Pantry. She operated her restaurant for a few years, and then she sold it at a profit to a business that turned the eatery into a corporate cafeteria. Next, Arline became one of the most successful travel agents in the country.

As a travel agent, Arline has shown that she can adapt with the best of them. Some years ago, the airlines decided that they were going to drop their commissions paid to travel agents down to a tough to live on zero percent. And they didn't

> *What could you do? You've been out of the job market for so long. And I said, "WATCH ME!"*

exactly give early notice. So what did Arline do? She built a hotel. She contracted with the Best Western people and put up a fifty-room hotel in Mentor, Ohio, to create another stream of revenue.

Arline bought the property for her hotel and travel agency with an original investment of forty-nine dollars. Yes, you read that right:

forty-nine dollars. Here's the story. Arline got a stock tip, which usually isn't a good reason to buy a stock, but she had a hunch. In the 1960s, when you could buy only a few shares of stock at a time, Arline took forty-nine dollars in birthday money, bought the stock, and forgot about it.

Years later, Arline learned that the company she had invested in was bought out. Her forty-nine dollar investment was now worth thousands. She used her windfall to buy the property needed for her new travel agency, hotel, century home, and upscale restaurant. It all started with a stock tip and a hunch.

When the World's Fair was in Montreal, Quebec, Canada, Arline recruited a large group of prospective clients who wanted to travel together. Her problem was finding an airline that was able to book a huge group on the same flight. Arline gave it some thought and simply chartered her own plane. Not only did this satisfy her clients' needs, but she wound up making a ton of money. That's Arline Kneen. The airlines gave her lemons, and she made lemonade. That's what entrepreneurs do. They think out of the box. They adapt!

When asked why she started all her companies, she said, "I was young enough, healthy enough, and stupid enough to think I could do it." But Arline admits that when things got tough, she would often pray, "Please God, I need your help."

It's an old saying, but when you are given lemons, make lemonade. Arline always adjusted. The good entrepreneurs are always able to pivot when they have to. That's one secret to her success.

Today, Arline gives all the credit for her success to the people she employs. She freely admits that without her children's support and her great staff, she never would have succeeded. Her son Rob and his wife Nancy do much of the work to make things happen. Rob says that his job is to get their businesses going until they have a "heartbeat" and start to grow.

Arline has no intention of stopping her travels any time soon. Traveling gives her the knowledge she needs in order to be the top agent on the block, and it's something she truly loves to do. Arline wants to experience everything the world has to offer. What's next for her at the young age of ninety-six? It's anyone's guess. She's probably planning her next venture now.

As Arline says, it takes good people to create a company, but it helps to have some birthday money and a "hunch" as well.

CHAPTER 24
Kip Marlow

Secrets to Success

Every entrepreneur has his or her own secrets to success. Targeting and hiring the right people, like an athletic team, is but one of them. However, to be a successful entrepreneur, here are the top five secrets gleaned from our radio interviews:

1. **Have passion, and do what you love**. All of the entrepreneurs in this book have that passion, some after operating their companies for twenty years. Barbie Gennarelli, founder of The Gourmet Soap Market, has a passion for scented soaps, and that passion drives her to succeed. Tim Blankenship, founder of Premier Dry Cleaners, loves what he does, and it drives him to succeed twenty-four hours a day, seven days a week. Without loving what you do, being an entrepreneur will be a lot harder, and your chances for success will be limited.

2. **Work hard.** Yes, it's a cliché, and it's overused, but it's a fundamental secret to every entrepreneur's success. Once you become a small business owner, you will be thinking about your business every hour of every day, even on vacations with your family. Working hard also means you constantly have to find a way to solve a problem or challenge, and sometimes that means you have to work around the clock. However, the rewards can be beyond your wildest dreams.

3. **Trust your instincts, but check your data.** As Roger Sustar, owner of Fredon Corporation, says, "Using your emotions is only good in love. Numbers don't lie." When you are bringing a new product to the market or making those vital hiring decisions, use your instincts but verify the data.

4. **Grasp those moments of destiny**. Tierra Destiny Reid was laid off, and this event became "the door that opened wide" for her to start her dream business. Dr. Ray Kralovic was fired from his job and ended up changing the world of surgical instrument sterilization. Jason Kintzler's wife, Jasmine, said, "When it's meant to be, it will happen." Jason won enough money playing the slots in Las Vegas to start Pitch Engine. All were moments of destiny, and these entrepreneurs recognized them, took action, and created companies.

5. **Be a continuous learner**. John Wooden, the famous college basketball coach, said that "it's what you learn after you know it all that counts." It's so true. We can have all the formal education we want, but learning starts in the "real world" of the marketplace. Most entrepreneurs read good business books or, at the very least, listen to them in their cars. Some even have mentors and join peer advisory groups. As Keith Kokal, founder of Micro Laboratories, says, he's always working, always looking, and always learning.

I trust that you enjoyed the book and were able to learn from our stories. All these entrepreneurs have been successful, but each struggled along the way. You will too. But these twenty-two success stories should encourage and inspire you to reach even greater heights and to build value and wealth for you and your family.

ACKNOWLEDGMENTS

Writing a book is very difficult, like becoming an entrepreneur. So just as in a business, it takes a team to make it all happen.

Many thanks to Ray Somich, owner of WELW Radio and welw.com, for granting me the privilege of air time for **Entrepreneurs Club Radio** and for writing the Foreword for this book.

Thanks as well to Kevin Patrick for his hard work in taking the shows' transcripts and writing many of the themes of each chapter.

Special thanks to all my radio guests. They are entrepreneurs, attorneys, marketing specialists, and time management specialists who help me encourage, inspire, and teach entrepreneurship every Monday.

21602402R00079

Made in the USA
Charleston, SC
25 August 2013